In this book, Alex, Ben, Kim and Danny want to solve some science puzzles. They all have different ideas. Can you help them answer their questions?

What do YOU think about our ideas? Do you have any other ideas? Why don't you talk to someone about what you think?

Ben

We'll show you how we try to find out the answers. You can try to find out too!

Alex

There are lots more ideas to try out at the back of the book.
Kim
Remember to check with a grown-up that what you're doing is safe.
Danny

A note to adults ▶

This book shows children that science is everywhere, and that they can find out about the world for themselves by thinking and investigating.

You can help children by reading the book with them and asking questions. At the start of each story, talk about what the characters are saying. While children are investigating, you could ask: What is happening? What can you see? Why do you think this is happening? Is it what you expected to happen? Children should be supervised while they are doing the investigations.

Each story ends with a simple explanation of what has happened. There are ideas for follow-up activities at the back of the book, and children may also want to find out more from other books, CD-Roms or the Internet.

Text copyright © 2000 Brenda and Stuart Naylor
Illustrations copyright © 2000 Ged Mitchell

Designed by Sarah Borny
Edited by Anne Clark

The rights of Brenda and Stuart Naylor and Ged Mitchell to be identified
as the authors and artist of this work have been asserted.

First published in 2000 by Hodder Children's Books,
a division of Hodder Headline,
338 Euston Road, London NW1 3BH

10 9 8 7 6 5 4 3 2 1

ISBN 0340 76444 9 Hardback
ISBN 0340 76445 7 Paperback
Printed in Hong Kong

Upside Down Seeds
and other science questions ▶

**Brenda and
Stuart Naylor**

Illustrated by
Ged Mitchell

*Hodder
Children's
Books*

a division of Hodder Headline

Upside Down Seeds

Alex, Danny and Kim are in the garden. They are growing some seeds. They want to make sure that the seeds grow properly.

It doesn't matter which way up they are.

Put them in the right way up!

But if they're upside down, the plants will grow upside down!
What do YOU think?
Let's find out more.

Ben will help you investigate.

1 ▶ Put some soil in three big pots. The pots need holes in the bottom.

2 ▶ Plant some seeds all the same way up in one pot. Then plant them different ways up in the other two pots. Label each pot.

3 Water the seeds and leave them until they grow. Give them more water if they get too dry.

4 Have all the seeds grown in the same way?

What did you find out?

The shoot of a seed always grows upwards. It doesn't matter which way up the seed is. If it is upside down then the shoot will still grow the right way round.

The Slide

There's a new slide in Kim's garden. Her little brother Sam is scared of going down too quickly. The children are wondering how they can slow him down.

Sam could sit on a paper towel.

Danny will help you investigate.

▶ 1 Use a smooth tray as a slide.

▶ 2 Put a thin sponge on the tray. Then put a teddy on top of the sponge.

▶ 3 Lift one end of the tray till the teddy starts to slide.

▶ 4 Try a paper towel on the tray.

5▶ Then try a piece of cardboard on the tray.

6▶ How high can you lift the tray each time before the teddy slides?

What did you find out?

Things which are rough or sticky don't usually slide well. Sponge is quite rough so it does not slide easily. Cardboard slides more easily because it is smoother.

Muddy Clothes

Ben, Alex and Danny are in a flap. Danny has fallen over playing football. His shirt is covered in mud.

Oh no! We'll have to wash your shirt in warm water.

Kim will help you investigate.

1 ▶ Mix soil and water to make some mud.

2 ▶ Rub the same amount of mud on four pieces of cloth.

3 ▶ Wash one piece in cold water and another in warm water.

4 Wash the third piece in cold water with soap, and the fourth in warm water with soap.

5 See which is the easiest to clean.

What did you find out? ▶

Dirt mixes more easily with water if the water is warm. Soap helps it mix even better. So we usually wash things with warm water and soap.

The Icy Path

It has been a cold and frosty night. There is ice all over the footpaths. The path by the house is very slippy.

Why don't we use salt to melt the ice?

Alex will help you investigate.

1 ▶ Ask a grown-up to take three ice cubes out of the freezer.

2 ▶ Sprinkle salt on one of the ice cubes.

3 ▶ Sprinkle sand or soil on the second ice cube.

4 Sprinkle sugar on the third.

5 Leave them for a while and see which ice cube melts most.

What did you find out?

It needs to be very, very cold to freeze salt and water when they are mixed together. When you put salt on ice, they mix and the ice melts.

Now you have started finding out, you might not want to stop!

Upside Down Seeds

What else might change the way the seeds grow? Does it matter if they are split in half? Does it make any difference if some are planted deeper in the soil than others?

The Slide

Try some more materials for yourself. Do some slide more easily than others? You could try sandpaper, corrugated paper, wool, rubber and polystyrene. Are there some surprises?